MAY

2008

Newsmakers™

Vladimir Putin

**President of
Russia**

Aaron Rosenberg

ROSEN
PUBLISHING®

New York

Published in 2008 by The Rosen Publishing Group, Inc.
29 East 21st Street, New York, NY 10010

First Edition

Library of Congress Cataloging-in-Publication Data

Rosenberg, Aaron.
Vladimir Putin: president of Russia/Aaron Rosenberg.
    p. cm.—(Newsmakers)
Includes bibliographical references and index.
ISBN-13: 978-1-4042-1903-8
ISBN-10: 1-4042-1903-X
1. Putin, Vladimir Vladimirovich (1952–)—Juvenile literature.
2. Presidents—Russia (Federation)—Biography—Juvenile literature.
I. Title.
DK510.766.P87R66 2007
947.086092—dc22

                                                    2006039726

Manufactured in the United States of America

On the cover: Vladimir Putin addresses reporters during a press conference with Vietnamese president Nguyen Minh Triet *(not pictured)* on November 20, 2006, on a Hanoi visit to discuss energy cooperation between their countries.

MAY 2008

CONTENTS

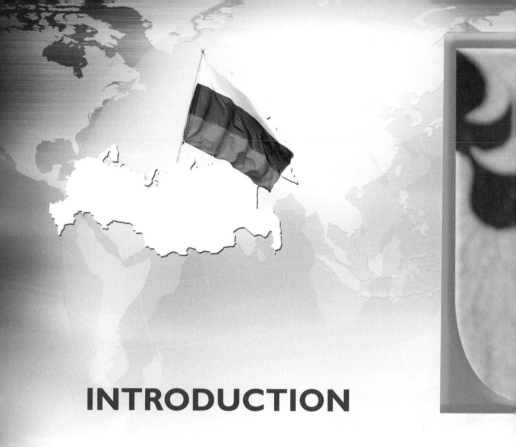

INTRODUCTION

For nearly seventy-five years, the Union of Soviet Socialist Republics (USSR), or Soviet Union, was one of the world's largest nations and, along with the United States, one of its two superpowers. However, by the mid-1980s, the Soviet Union had become critically unstable. It faced an ailing economy and its government was rife with corruption and internal conflict. Various factions fought for control, and its leader, Mikhail Gorbachev, began devising different ways to run the country. After negotiations, a treaty for a new union emerged. It was designed to

Vladimir Putin gives a speech from his press office in the Kremlin during the 2006 People's Unity Day celebrations in Moscow. People's Unity day is observed on November 4.

establish each Soviet republic's independence under a single presidency, scheduled for signing on August 20, 1991.

In opposition to increasing the power of the republics, a group of KGB Communist hardliners, the Extraordinary Commission, staged a coup in Moscow the day before the treaty was to be signed. Boris Yeltsin, who had become Russia's first popularly elected president just two months earlier, vehemently defied this group and successfully corralled the public's support in his favor. The coup folded within days, but Gorbachev never regained power. He stepped down from his office on Christmas Day that year, and the Soviet Union dissolved into its fifteen independent states.

As the most powerful state, Russia assumed the Soviet Union's former roles at the Kremlin, with Yeltsin as its president. Under his adminis-tration, the country's economy, despite early signs of recuperation, plummeted further. Many believe Yeltsin's economic reforms for privatization took place too quickly and were instituted without caution.

Facing mercilessly low approval ratings and racked by illness, Yeltsin resigned and selected a successor, Vladimir Putin, whom he had recently installed as prime minister. With Yeltsin's support, Putin easily won the election in 2000, becoming Russia's second president. He has remained in office since, winning a second term in 2004.

But what do we really know about this man? Before Yeltsin's endorsement, few people outside

Russia had even heard of Putin. Who is this man currently in charge of one of the world's largest nations?

To many, Putin is an enigma. To others, he is a controversial leader. He appeared from nowhere to take control of Russia, and his calm, quiet manner has left many baffled. But Putin is no newcomer to politics, or to Russia's problems. He has been in politics for many years. Before that he was part of the KGB, the Soviet Union's intelligence agency, and spent several years in the former East Germany. Many refer to Putin as the "Grey Cardinal." He is reserved and quietly determined, not boldly outspoken and brash like his predecessor Yeltsin. Also, some allege that he held considerable power behind the scenes before his election to the presidency.

By looking at his life, we can learn more about Putin's character and better understand this powerful political leader. It is equally important to explore the political, economic, and cultural forces that shaped the country in which he was raised and rose to power.

CHAPTER ONE

HUMBLE BEGINNINGS, GREAT AMBITIONS

Vladimir Vladimirovich Putin was born on October 7, 1952, in Leningrad. (Originally St. Petersburg, the city's name was changed to Leningrad in 1924 to posthumously honor Vladimir Lenin. It reverted back to St. Petersburg after the Soviet Union's collapse in 1991.) His father, Vladimir Spirdonovich Putin, had been born there as well, in 1911. Putin's grandfather had been a chef who cooked not only for Lenin, but also for Joseph Stalin after him. His grandfather even claimed to have served Rasputin as a boy. After World War I, the family moved to the village of Pominovo, in the Tver region. Putin's father met a young woman named Maria and they were married. They were seventeen at the time. Shortly after their marriage, Putin's father entered the army. He served on a submarine fleet and completed his term of service without incident.

In 1932, the young couple moved back to St. Petersburg and settled into the suburb of Peterhof. They had two sons years before Vladimir was born, and one died after only a few months. When World War II began, Putin's father, Vladimir Sr., volunteered to return to the front. He was assigned to a demolitions unit. Putin's mother, Maria, stayed in their home in Peterhof. Her brother served at the naval head-quarters in St. Petersburg and took her and her surviving son in to keep them safe. However, the child died of diphtheria during Germany's siege of Leningrad, which began September 9, 1941, and ended January 18, 1944. During this very harsh time, Maria almost succumbed to starvation while her brother was stationed elsewhere.

Putin's father was routinely sent behind German lines to sabotage buildings and other important locations. He and his unit took control of the Neva Nickel, a small circular area along the Neva River. It was there that he was badly wounded with shrapnel in both legs. He could have died, but a Russian soldier, who happened

German forces placed Leningrad under siege for 900 days during World War II. In this 1942 photo, besieged Leningrad citizens scoop up water from a broken main.

to be an old family friend, found him and carried him across the frozen Neva to the rest of the Russian troops. It was many months before Vladimir Sr. was well enough to leave the hospital, and he limped for the rest of his life.

YOUNG VOLODYA

After the war, Putin's father was given a job as a toolmaker in the Yegorov Train Car Factory. His

mother worked as a janitor, delivered bakery
products, and cleaned test tubes in a laboratory.
The factory where his father worked furnished
them with a small room in a communal apartment
in the center of St. Petersburg. Putin was born
there. His birth was considered a miracle
because his mother was forty-one at the time,
suffered poor health for years, and had already
lost two very young sons.

Vladimir Putin, or young "Volodya," spent his
childhood running around the building and playing
in its narrow inner courtyard. They lived on the
fifth floor and had no elevator. The stairwell
was infested with rats, which Volodya chased
with sticks. The rooms of their apartment were
dim and cramped. The tiny kitchen was equally
confining, and they had no running hot water or
even a bathtub. The Putins shared the apartment
with an elderly Jewish couple and their unmarried
daughter. Despite the arguments the Putins had
with them, the couple treated Volodya like a son.

One of their neighbors, an old woman
named Baba Anya, was devout in her Russian
Orthodox beliefs and regularly attended church.

The Communist Party of the Soviet Union (CPSU)

After the Russian Revolution of 1917 and the end of tsarist rule, the Bolsheviks rose to power under Vladimir Lenin's leadership and established the Soviet Union, the world's first Communist nation. Amid anti-Communist resistance, the Russian Civil War (1917–1921) ensued, during which the Bolsheviks instituted "war communism." This policy was meant to sustain the production of goods and Communist troops, and nationalized private property and industries, creating the template of state control of the Soviet economy for years to come. Warding off anti-Communists and rivaling factions, the Bolsheviks eventually became known as the Communist Party of the Soviet Union in 1952, the year Putin was born. Under the CPSU and the iron fist of totalitarian leader Joseph Stalin, the Soviet Union had become a formidable world power and an authoritarian state in which civil liberties and individual rights were all but eradicated. However, by 1991, the CPSU broke up when Mikhail Gorbachev, the party's final leader, attempted to decentralize the country's political and economic systems, resulting in the collapse of the Soviet Union.

She influenced Putin's mother, who in turn became religious and had young Vladimir baptized. However, they did not tell his father, as he would not have approved. Putin's father was a member of the Communist Party of the Soviet Union (CPSU) and the secretary of the factory's party organization. The Russian Orthodox faith was officially banned by the CPSU, although many still practiced it in secret. It was many years before Putin could openly admit to his faith.

GAINING SELF-DISCIPLINE

Young Vladimir spent all his time at home until he started school when he was nearly eight years old. Though school was only a few buildings away, putting on and buttoning up the coat always made him late. To avoid that, he stopped wearing the coat altogether. He would simply run to and from class as fast as possible.

Vladimir was a bright child, and those around him recognized his potential, but he lacked self-discipline. Some of his teachers remembered him as quiet and distant, even inattentive. (Other than German, he did not

show interest in his other studies.) Therefore, he received low, albeit passing, marks in school. He was far more interested in making friends and gaining a position of authority among his fellow students. In fact, Putin describes his childhood self as a hooligan.

Most Soviet children belonged to a club called the Young Pioneers; membership, though not required, was strongly encouraged. Young Pioneers were eligible for activities such as attending state-run camps and taking special classes. However, Vladimir did not join until the sixth grade—he was too undisciplined and rebellious to be accepted before that.

However, athletics helped Vladimir turn his life around. Around the age of ten, he realized he needed more skills if he planned to keep fighting

A young Vladimir Putin (bottom) wrestles with a classmate at the St. Petersburg Sports School in 1971. Putin later abandoned wrestling for sambo and then judo.

other kids at school. He took up boxing but got his nose broken almost immediately. The pain was immense, and Vladimir couldn't bring himself to try boxing again.

So when he was fourteen, he began practicing sambo, a Soviet martial art, and joined the Trud athletic club, which practiced at a local gym. Unexpectedly, his coach announced that the class would be switching from sambo to judo. Judo is a philosophy as much as a sport, emphasizing discipline, respect, and patience.

Vladimir took to judo quickly, applied himself to it, and began winning matches within a year. He also stopped causing trouble at home and in school—his grades even showed improvement. At first, his parents had disapproved of judo, until they met Vladimir's coach and saw how the martial art was helping to instill their son with a sense of direction.

A SECRET GOAL

Early in life, Vladimir longed to become a pilot. The Academy of Civil Aviation was in Leningrad, and he eagerly read its brochures and subscribed to an aviation journal.

However, later in his youth, Vladimir became fascinated with Soviet spy books and movies, which were very popular in the country at the time. In particular, *The Shield and the Sword*, a book (and subsequent movie) about a Soviet spy in Nazi Germany, struck a chord with Vladimir so deeply that he decided to become a secret agent instead of a pilot. He was intrigued by the idea that a single man, as a successful spy, could accomplish more than an entire army.

In the Soviet Union, being a spy meant working for the KGB, the nation's intelligence agency. Vladimir devoured everything he could about the agency and about spies in general. Then, at the start of the ninth grade, Vladimir set off for the local KGB office. He asked the official there what he had to do in order to join.

The official told Vladimir two things. First, the KGB did not accept volunteers, but sought out potential members. Second, he said that Vladimir would either need to enlist in the army or earn a college degree. Vladimir asked what degree was best, and the official told him the KGB preferred law students. From then on, Vladimir aspired for law school, with the intention of working for the KGB.

His parents did not understand this shift in his ambitions. As a talented athlete, Vladimir stood a very good chance of becoming a pilot. His coach believed he could probably get into the Academy of Civil Aviation, but Vladimir wanted to go to Leningrad State University, which would lead to law school. According to Professor Valery Musin, a former lecturer at the university, its law department operated as a place to train KGB agents.

Vladimir knew he could not mention his goal without attracting the KGB's attention, which would effectively ruin his chance of being recruited, so he kept it a secret. Unaware of his motives for law school, his parents and coach tried to talk him out his new plan, as competition to enter the university was fierce. It took only a handful of students straight from high school—

most of its admission slots were reserved for soldiers. If Vladimir failed to be admitted, he would have to join the army or go to a technical school. However, these factors did not deter him from pursuing his secret ambition. Vladimir concentrated on his studies, excelled at judo, and gained acceptance to Leningrad State University after graduating from high school in 1970.

AT UNIVERSITY

In college, Putin proved to be a studious pupil, hardly indulging in any vices. He did not drink much and abstained from smoking. Moreover, he rarely went to parties and he never gambled. His academic studies came first. Judo came second.

He also had little money. One summer, Putin worked in construction, which paid well, but he and his friends spent most of their earnings quickly. He did have a car—which was a real luxury—because his mother bought a lottery ticket one day and won it. She gave it to Putin even though she could have sold it for a good deal of money. Putin loved the car and drove it

This is the main building of St. Petersburg State University, where Putin earned his law degree. The university was founded by Peter the Great on January 28, 1724.

everywhere, showing a taste for speed. He was a conscientious driver, however, as he would not be able to pay for repairs if he had an accident.

Putin remained dedicated to the practice of martial arts. He became a sambo black belt shortly after starting college. Two years later, he became a judo master. Several coaches urged him to join their teams, but Putin remained with Trud. In 1974, he won the citywide judo competition. The competition included amateurs, professionals, and several European and Olympic champions. Almost three decades later, Putin would go on to co-author and publish a book on judo.

He also started dating a young woman and got engaged to her. She was a medical student, and both their families approved. But out of nowhere, Putin called the marriage off just before the ceremony. He has never said why, only that it was complicated. It is possible that he worried about what might happen to his spouse and their marriage if he joined the KGB.

THE RECRUITMENT

The KGB often recruited college students to spy on their fellow students, but they never approached Putin. Worry set in, and he began to consider the option of becoming a prosecutor. Nonetheless, in his fourth year in college, someone approached Putin. He would not reveal the organization for whom he worked, but he expressed interest in Putin's career plans. He knew immediately that this mysterious individual represented the KGB and intended to recruit him. Putin's excitement ran high, though he did not show it.

After graduating from the International Department of the Law Faculty of Leningrad State University in 1975, Putin immediately reported to the KGB. This was what he had been working toward for years. He had a romantic idea of the intelligence community, based on the Soviet espionage movies he had seen and books he had read. Putin imagined a life of daring adventure and thrilling missions. However, the reality of working for the KGB would prove to be much different than his expectations.

CHAPTER TWO

LIFE WITH THE KGB

P utin began his career with the KGB in the Secretariat of the Directorate, where he was placed in the counterintelligence division. Working for the agency was a shock. Putin had expected his career to resemble the ones in the movies and books he had loved in his youth. Instead, he found himself bogged down in an office, working with men nearing retirement. His coworkers followed the KGB's instructions precisely, even when their actions were not lawful; Soviet intelligence was essentially above the law. Having come a long way from his troubled childhood, Putin did not understand their conduct.

Putin trained and worked in counterintelligence for six months. The different agencies within the KGB were always looking to claim the best new members for themselves. During his first few months, Putin had caught the eye of several foreign intelligence officers. Foreign intelligence was considered the most desirable division. Its

The KGB

The Komitet Gosudarstvennoy Bezopasnosti (Committee of State Security) was founded in 1954. It was the Soviet Union's state security organization, as well as the nation's secret police and intelligence agency. The KGB grew out of the All-Russian Extraordinary Commission for Combating Counterrevolution and Sabotage (Cheka), an intelligence organization founded by Felix Dzerhinsky in 1917 to protect the new Soviet Union from foreign threats. The Cheka evolved into several other organizations, including the Ministry for State Security (MGB) and the Russian Ministry of Internal Affairs (MVD). The MGB and the MVD merged in 1953, but were split again a year later into a reduced MVD and the newly established KGB. The KGB was responsible for internal and external security, including protecting leaders and guarding currency. For many years, it was the largest espionage organization in the world, feared by Soviet citizens and other nations. It was dismantled in 1991, after its leaders took part in the failed Soviet coup.

agents traveled abroad, earned a great deal of prestige, and were paid very well. In spite of this, many used their positions to trade in foreign goods, either by acquiring items abroad and selling them personally back home, or by using their connections to arrange shipments and sales. This was illegal, but very profitable; because of economic decline in the Soviet Union, most agents made money where they could.

Working in foreign intelligence appealed to Putin, so when the officers offered him a place in their division, he accepted. They sent him to Moscow for a year of special training, and upon completion, Putin reported to the "first department." This was the intelligence branch.

For four and a half years, Putin worked for the first department and earned the esteem of both his superiors and peers. Afterward, he was sent to the Andropov Red Banner Institute in Moscow for additional training as an agent. Putin arrived there already a KGB major and was quickly made a division leader, impressing his instructors with his diligence, discipline, organization, and tact. In spite of this, Putin did have a few marks against him. Many of his instructors felt he was too reserved, showing tendencies to be withdrawn and uncommunicative. His other qualities more than compensated, however, and Putin was approved to become a foreign intelligence agent.

STARTING A FAMILY

Putin went through two major changes during this time. First, he joined the CPSU, the Communist Party. This was not a matter of choice—every member of the Soviet intelligence community was required to become a party member. Putin had no particular interest in Communism, but he was a loyal citizen and a diligent worker.

The second major change was meeting a young woman named Lyudmila Aleksandrovna. She was a flight attendant from Kaliningrad.

This spring 1985 photo shows Vladimir Putin; his wife, Lyudmila; and their baby daughter, Masha. They moved to Dresden, East Germany, soon after.

Lyudmila and a girlfriend had flown to Leningrad for three days. Her friend met a young man, who invited her to a performance by the comedian Arkady Raikin. She asked Lyudmila to go with her. The young man brought a friend as well— Vladimir Putin. Vladimir and Lyudmila got along well and went out the next two nights. Thanks to his KGB connections, Putin was able to get them tickets to events each night.

On the third night, Putin gave Lyudmila his phone number, which surprised his friend. He had seen Putin with girls before, but had never seen him give any of them much personal information. The soon-to-be couple spoke on the phone several times, and Lyudmila began flying down to Leningrad to see him. Putin did not tell her he worked with the KGB, however. He told her he was with the police, in criminal investigation. All KGB members had a cover story; they were unable to reveal to anyone that they worked in intelligence.

Vladimir and Lyudmila spent the next three and a half years dating before he proposed to her, as he was hesitant to rush into such commitment. She said yes, and they were married three months later. Both took their wedding vows seriously, believing that marriage was a major responsibility and something no one should enter into without careful consideration.

After their marriage, Vladimir and Lyudmila moved in with his parents. Putin's father had been given a three-room apartment because he was a disabled war veteran. Vladimir and Lyudmila took the middle room for themselves. The couples lived in close quarters, but they got along well with each other. Having dropped out of technical college to become a flight attendant, Lyudmila went back to school after she and Putin started dating. She entered Leningrad State University and enrolled in language studies.

In her fourth year of school, Lyudmila gave birth to their first daughter, Masha. The family had little time to celebrate, however, as they were too busy packing. Putin had just returned from his year in the Andropov Institute. He had passed the exams and had been approved. Now he had been given his first foreign service post. Lyudmila had also been issued security clearance. Without it, she would not have been able to accompany her husband. But the KGB had talked to her professors and friends, approving her for travel.

The family was going to Dresden, a city in East Germany, which was a Soviet ally. At the time, the Soviet Union stationed 380,000 troops and stored missiles in Dresden.

THE TRANSFER

The family arrived in Dresden in 1986, and Lyudmila graduated from college. Masha was a year old, and the Putins were expecting their second child.

Putin began his post in Dresden coordinating with the Stasi, the German secret police. His job was to gather political intelligence. This meant obtaining and analyzing information about the Soviet Union's political opponents. The North Atlantic Treaty Organization (NATO) was considered the primary opponent at the time. He also recruited information sources.

This was an important part of the process, requiring Putin to find reliable sources and establish relationships with them.

At this point in his career, Putin was a senior case officer, a position that he has described as routine. Still, he earned two promotions. First, he became assistant to the head of the department, then he advanced to senior assistant. He was also appointed to the CPSU committee of the KGB representation in East Germany. Some reports claim he was involved in technical acquisitions and helped to steal Western technology, which Putin denies. He says he never had access to such information and was not assigned to seek it, that his information was strictly political and dealt with people and parties.

The Putins' second daughter, Katya, was born shortly after they arrived, and they settled into their new home. Life in Dresden was good in some ways. The family had a nice place to live, in a building with the rest of the Soviet agents and several of the Stasi agents and their families. Masha and Katya were provided day care with the other children from their building. They were spared food shortages and the streets were clean. With their car, the family even took weekend drives in the country. Putin put on several pounds—he began to drink beer regularly and did not exercise much.

Nonetheless, the Putins were homesick. In some ways, East Germany was far more repressive than the Soviet Union. Its people were under strict control and constant surveillance. To Putin, it was reminiscent of the Soviet Union thirty years earlier, during Stalin's horrible purges, when merely questioning authority risked imprisonment or death. As foreigners, Putin and his family also felt isolated. Although they made friends, became fluent in German, and stayed there for four years, they never felt completely at home.

THE FALL OF THE WALL

In 1989, Putin watched a crowd of East Germans break into the East German Ministry of Security (MGB). They had reached a breaking point with the scrutinizing and restrictive policies of their country. For Putin, this was a frightening

Soviet president Mikhail Gorbachev *(center)* speaks to a crowd of Soviet delegates during the 28th Community Party Congress in 1990. The Soviet Union collapsed a year later.

experience. Many of the MGB workers were friends of his, and he and his colleagues worried that their offices would also be targeted. Therefore, they destroyed many of their documents and sent the rest to Moscow for safekeeping.

The crowd began to grow and the situation intensified, so Putin went outside to speak with them. They were angry and demanded to know what he was doing there. He addressed them in fluent German, which made them uncomfortable. Sensing this, Putin and his coworkers began to worry that they would be attacked.

Concerns for their safety escalated, prompting Putin to call the local Soviet military leader. He explained the situation and asked for troops to protect them and their families. He was told that they could do nothing without authorization from Moscow. A few hours later, the East German military finally arrived and the crowd dispersed. Still, the fact that Moscow did not immediately act shook Putin badly. He felt it was a clear sign of instability in the Soviet Union, where tensions between Moscow and the republics seeking more independence were mounting. Also, perestroika, Gorbachev's economic reforms, had the unintended effect of worsening the shortages of food and other necessities. The angry public, encouraged by glasnost (a policy that helped to increase the freedom of speech), voiced its opinions more openly than ever.

With their eyes on Moscow, the German people began protesting and rioting for change and for freedom. Consequently, in October 1989, East German leader Erich Honecker was removed from office. The entire East German cabinet stepped down on November 7. Two days later, all travel restrictions were lifted. Masses of people immediately gathered at the Berlin Wall, which separated East and West Germany, and began to tear it down. East Germany had fallen.

Putin and his colleagues knew their work in Germany was finished. They could no longer remain there safely. They severed all ties with their contacts and sources, packed up their remaining files, and headed home.

For the Putins, it was a difficult time. They had to leave their comfortable life behind. Food shortages and long lines for everything awaited them in the Soviet Union. They were also affected by the suffering experienced by their East German friends, most of whom were affiliated with the Stasi or the MGB. Many West Germans looked down on their eastern cousins (who

were less educated and prepared to cope with dramatic change after years of repression), and taunted, insulted, and humiliated them. Those from East German intelligence were particularly singled out.

But nothing could be done. Putin had worked in conjunction with East German intelligence, and now East Germany no longer existed. His office's agreements were no longer relevant. The Putins had no other choice but to return to Leningrad.

A German officer helps a guard step through an opening in the Berlin Wall on November 11, 1989, shortly after East Germany lifted its restrictions against traveling to the west.

CHAPTER THREE

THE GREY CARDINAL

U pon his return to the Soviet Union, Putin was offered a post at the central office in Moscow. But he had begun to lose faith in the KGB and felt let down by his country, so he declined. Putin worked diligently to procure information in East Germany, and he and his colleagues sent Moscow reports on the unrest in Dresden and suggestions on how to ease the situation. However, his superiors in Moscow made no attempt to act on the intelligence Putin provided.

Still, Putin had a wife and two young children, and he could not afford to abandon his career. He had no intention of going to Moscow, so he continued to work for the KGB in Leningrad. It gave him an opportunity to go back to Leningrad State University, undercover as a returning student. Putin's superiors expected him to report if he noticed anything dangerous or unusual, a condition to which he agreed. His status with the KGB changed, and he became an "active reserve" officer. In 1990, he became assistant to the president of the university, and as far as Putin was concerned, his life as an agent was over. He began work on a doctoral dissertation and planned to stay at the university, both as a student and as staff.

Though a level of stability was returned to their lives, the Putins had little money. They had not been able to save much during their time in Germany, and life in Leningrad was more difficult than ever. After such easy access to food in Dresden, the long lines and use of ration cards in Leningrad were hard to bear.

WORKING FOR SOBCHAK

Putin began work on his dissertation, choosing international private law as his topic. Several of his old friends from his university days had joined the faculty at Leningrad State University. One of them, a professor, asked Putin for a favor. He was friends with Anatoly Aleksandrovich Sobchak, the chair of the Leningrad City Council. Sobchak was a powerful local politician

Anatoly Sobchak attends a press conference in Moscow on December 7, 1993. The bull on the poster behind him symbolized the country's democratic movement for reform.

and once taught at the university. In fact, Putin had been in one of his classes. Most local politicians were corrupt, and the professor felt Sobchak needed someone especially trustworthy on his team. Therefore, he asked Putin to step in as Sobchak's assistant.

Putin agreed to meet with Sobchak, who immediately approved of Putin and offered him the position. Though he unofficially retired from intelligence work, Putin made sure Sobchak knew he was a KGB officer. This did not sway Sobchak, and when Putin told his superiors at the KGB about the job offer, they approved.

As Sobchak's assistant, Putin was loyal and soon earned his trust. Even when the KGB approached Putin about securing Sobchak's approval for a KGB-supported proposal, Putin refused. The KGB did not press the matter, but several city council deputies began pressuring Putin. They threatened to expose his intelligence ties unless he helped them win Sobchak's support for their own projects. The public did not trust the KGB and considered anyone from the agency to be a spy, a saboteur, or an assassin loyal only to Communist Party leaders.

It was a difficult decision for Putin. The KGB had still been paying him a salary, on which he and his family depended. There was also no guarantee Sobchak would remain in office. If he failed, Putin would lose his position as well, and once he left the KGB, Putin could never go back.

Ultimately, Putin no longer felt comfortable being an undercover agent, and he submitted his letter of resignation. Next, with a friend who was a film director, he taped an interview concerning his background with the KGB, intending that it would be broadcast publicly. As a result, the interview aired on Leningrad television. Putin's intelligence ties were revealed, and the city council deputies could no longer blackmail him.

In 1991, Mikhail Gorbachev negotiated a new union treaty. It would make the Soviet republics significantly more independent. A less fixed federation would unite them under a single president, shared military, and common foreign policy. Many Communists were opposed to this as it would decentralize state power. Gorbachev was set to sign the treaty on August 20. However, the day before, the newly formed Extraordinary Commission announced that Gorbachev was ill and had been removed from office. In reality, he was on vacation and placed under house arrest by the Extraordinary Commission. The commission, lead by KGB chief Vladimir Kryuchkov, attempted to gain control in Moscow, but it met with fierce

In Moscow's Manege Square, Russian soldiers sit atop their armored personnel carrier and ignore taunts from protesters during the August 19, 1991, coup by Soviet hardliners.

resistance, especially from Boris Yeltsin. He was the most outspoken opponent, and his strong words solidified public opposition. The coup failed and, on August 21, Gorbachev had returned to office. However, he was no longer in control. By early December, the Soviet Union was collapsing. Gorbachev resigned as president on December 25, and the Soviet flag was lowered and removed. The Russian flag was raised in its place.

Putin was on vacation when the 1991 coup against Gorbachev began. He hurried back to the city. On August 20, he and Sobchak moved into the City Council offices along with several colleagues.

Putin had already resigned from the KGB and was no longer required to obey its orders, but his letter of resignation had disappeared unsigned. The commission issued orders to all KGB members. Putin could be tried for treason if he disobeyed. Fortunately, Sobchak called Kryuchkov himself. Kryuchkov confirmed Putin's resignation and Putin was no longer in danger.

A NEW POST

In 1991, Sobchak created the Committee for Foreign Liaison, appointing Putin as its head. The committee worked to bring more foreign trade to St. Petersburg—the city had changed its name back from Leningrad after the Soviet

Union's collapse. The committee also encouraged Western banks to open local branches and upgraded the city's infrastructure. They brought in Coca-Cola and other foreign investors, even opening a faculty of international relations at the university so workers could learn foreign languages.

It was a very busy time for Putin. He was working long hours and was rarely home. Even when not at work, he seemed lost in thought, pacing frequently. He had become caught up in politics and in trying to make St. Petersburg a better place.

Making matters more complicated, Putin and Sobchak agreed that the City Council was threatened by instability. Sobchak was chair, but could be removed by the other council members at any time. If he and Putin were going to continue protecting and improving St. Petersburg, they would need a more secure office. Putin convinced Sobchak and the council deputies to create the new post of mayor. With Putin's help, Sobchak was elected mayor in 1992. Sobchak made Putin his deputy mayor.

SOBCHAK'S DEFEAT

In 1996, Sobchak faced a second mayoral election. In 1992, he had been the clear favorite. This election was different, however, as other politicians had seen how the office worked. They had spent the last four years watching and learning, and now they were ready to campaign for office. Putin warned Sobchak that he would need professional campaign managers this time around, but Sobchak decided to run the campaign himself.

This proved to be a disaster, as Sobchak was not prepared for his opponents' underhanded tactics. They spread negative impressions about him and accused him of crimes. None of these impressions or accusations were true, but Sobchak's opponents succeeded in tarnishing his reputation. Furthermore, Putin could not be of much help. Sobchak had left him in charge of city affairs during the campaign, and Putin was also working for the St. Petersburg headquarters of Boris Yeltsin's presidential campaign.

As a result, Sobchak lost the election. One of his rivals, Vladimir Yakovlev, was elected mayor. In reaction, Putin left his post as deputy mayor. He was unwilling to stay behind and work for one of Sobchak's rivals, and, with his family, he moved up to the country house they had built a few years before.

Six weeks later, the Putins' house burned to the ground; the builders had incorrectly installed the stove in the banya. Because the builders were at fault, the Putins did not have to pay for rebuilding it. This took a year and a half, and their house was built to the exact specifications of the first one.

A POWERFUL MAN BEHIND THE SCENES

Putin maintained contact with officials in Moscow after the St. Petersburg mayoral election. Having worked industriously for Yeltsin's campaign, he earned the favor of several powerful officials and they assured Putin of future employment. However, placing him proved to be an obstacle. Initially, Putin was offered a post as deputy to the chief of the presidential administration, but when the department was reorganized, the post was eliminated. Then, he was offered a position with the Directorate for Public Liaison. But just as Putin was submitting his acceptance, Chief of Staff Pavel Borodin offered to make him his deputy instead. Putin found this new, unexpected career opportunity considerably more appealing and accepted it without hesitation.

In August 1996, Putin and his family moved to Moscow. Settling into a beautiful older home, the Putins quickly grew to love the city, which they felt was more cosmopolitan than St. Petersburg.

After his arrival in Moscow, Putin made several key career advances. In 1997, he was appointed head of the Main Control Directorate, an important but unappealing post for him. A year later, he became first deputy head of the presidential administration, responsible for the

Lyudmila Putin visits her native town of Kaliningrad on September 8, 2000, and signs autographs for school-children at School 8, where she was once a student.

regions and liaisons with its governors. Putin particularly enjoyed working with the governors and building relationships around the country.

A few months later, Putin was appointed to a new post: director of the Federal Security Service (FSB), Russia's post-Soviet intelligence agency. Putin did not seek the position; President Yeltsin simply placed him there. For Putin, it was an undesired return to a world of surveillance and scrutiny. He was offered the rank of general so that he could command the agents more easily, since all active agents had a military rank. Putin declined it, however, becoming the first civilian director of the security agencies. At this time, he was also made secretary of the Security Council.

Though he quickly broke through the ranks, Putin kept himself in the shadows. Most government officials knew of him, but the Russian public did not. Some of Putin's colleagues referred to him as a "grey cardinal," meaning a man who has power but uses it quietly from behind the scenes.

During his farewell ceremony, resigning Russian president Boris Yeltsin shakes hands with the newly appointed acting President Vladimir Putin on December 31, 1999, at the Kremlin.

Then, in August 1999, Putin gained a crucial advancement—Yeltsin appointed him prime minister. Yeltsin seemed unable to keep anyone in the position, as Putin was made Russia's fifth prime minister in eighteen months. Putin himself did not expect to retain the post for long.

Hence, he felt at liberty to respond decisively to
the crisis in Chechnya, indifferent to any potential
political or public backlash. Surprisingly, this swift
maneuver won Putin the support of the Unity
Party. The party took the majority in the Duma
(Russian parliament) elections that December,
and Putin was reappointed prime minister.

Suddenly, it seemed as if Putin might have a
long political career after all, and he became
widely viewed as Yeltsin's probable successor.
The presidential elections were due to occur the
following summer. But on December 31, 1999,
Boris Yeltsin unexpectedly resigned from the
presidency. Following the established protocols,
Putin became acting president of the Russian
Federation.

CHAPTER FOUR

THE REFORMER

Putin has claimed in interviews that he did not initially desire the presidency. Yeltsin had called him into the presidential office a few weeks before New Year's and abruptly informed him about his plan to resign, leaving Putin to become acting president. He told Yeltsin he was unsure of his readiness for assuming such a position of leadership. However, Putin was a pragmatist and did not hesitate to take office.

One of his first acts was to reschedule the presidential elections. They were planned for the next summer, but Putin moved them up to spring, which meant his opponents had little time to prepare. The election was held on March 26, and Putin won with 53 percent of the vote. He was inaugurated as the second president of the Russian Federation on May 7, 2000, becoming Russia's youngest leader since Joseph Stalin took control in 1922.

Vladimir Putin speaks to journalists on March 15, 2000, from his campaign headquarters near the Kremlin immediately after he easily won his bid for re-election.

PUTIN'S NEW GOVERNMENT

Without further delay, Putin shaped his administration. He retained several of Yeltsin's chief advisors and top officials, but he brought in new members, including several friends and former colleagues from St. Petersburg. Many of them were economic reformers and law experts, indicative of the major changes Putin planned to implement.

Russia has eighty-nine separate political territories, including Moscow and St. Petersburg. During his presidency, Yeltsin had allowed all of them increased autonomy, which counter-productively reduced communication and cooperation between territorial and regional leaders and Moscow. To strengthen these links, Putin organized the country into seven super-regions and appointed a plenipotentiary representative for each one. These representatives coordinated activities between their own region, other regions, and the central government. This strategy harkened back to Putin's own work with Yeltsin's presidential administration, where he emphasized communication between regional leaders and the Kremlin. Critics complained that Putin's representatives were all former KGB officers and former military leaders, and were wary that these representatives intended to control the regions rather than coordinate with them.

Putin also revised the Federation Council. This upper house of the Duma had included governors and heads of the regional legislatures. Putin replaced them with new representatives, permitting them to concentrate on their own regions while regulating their individual powers. Critics argued, however, that he had weakened the council and rigged the elections to undermine the governors who politically opposed him.

BREAKING DOWN THE OLIGARCHS

After the dissolution of the Soviet Union, many state businesses became privately owned. The financial leaders who took control of those businesses accrued immense wealth and power. Many of them had been government officials and used their connections to gain company control and favorable government contracts. As a result, corruption rose to unprecedented levels. Many Russians felt that these businessmen, or oligarchs, essentially ran the country, using their wealth and influence to sway politicians as a means for personal gain.

Moreover, Yeltsin's administration was in step with this corruption. Many members of the

"Family," as his inner circle was called, worked for or had ties with the oligarchs. Most Family members grew rich on bribes and kickbacks, and Yeltsin himself was suspected of corruption, accused of money laundering by both Russian and Swiss authorities.

Putin had been part of the Family himself—no one advanced to prime minister without such connections. When he became president, many assumed he would allow the oligarchs to continue as Yeltsin had. To Putin, however, they were little more than criminals flaunting their ability to break laws and control officials. Subsequently, he targeted the most powerful oligarchs and set out to break down their political control.

Putin's first target was Vladimir Gusinsky. Gusinsky controlled one of the nation's largest media companies and had helped fund Yeltsin's 1996 presidential campaign. In return, Gusinsky was awarded many lucrative government contracts, and a state-controlled company oversaw and excused his financial debts. As president, Putin had Gusinsky arrested for embezzling state property. He then forced

Gusinsky to surrender his business interests, ultimately exiling him. Putin also went after Boris Berezovsky. Berezovsky had been part of the Family and assisted in Putin's rise to power. Nonetheless, Putin wanted this oligarch gone. To avoid a fate similar to Gusinsky's, Berezovsky fled the country to dodge embezzlement charges, and the government seized his assets.

With Gusinsky and Berezovsky out of the picture, the other oligarchs feared for their wealth and freedom. Sensing this advantage, Putin made an unofficial deal with them: the oligarchs could keep their assets, control of their companies, and evade the charges leveled at their cronies on the condition that they withdraw completely from politics. That meant ceasing the bribes, kickbacks, and financing of political candidates. Most oligarchs complied.

Oil baron Mikhail Khodorkovsky resisted, however. He was Russia's richest man and controlled the Yukos oil company. Despite Putin's demands, Khodorkovsky declared that he would finance several opposing political parties. In response, Putin arrested one of his partners, but

Demonstrators in St. Petersburg hold a caricature of Vladimir Putin and a photo of oligarch Mikhail Khodorkovsky, who was three years into his nine-year prison term, on April 27, 2006.

Khodorkovsky continued to financially back Putin's political rivals. Consequently, in fall 2003, he was arrested in Siberia, while his private jet was being refueled, and diverted to Moscow. There, Khodorkovsky was put on trial, convicted of fraud and tax evasion, and sentenced to nine years in prison. Yukos was heavily fined and broken up, with most of its former assets placed under state control.

Respect for the Soviet Past

Boris Yeltsin had spent much of his presidency attacking old rivals. He particularly detested the Communists and wanted every sign of Russia's Soviet past erased. He charged many of the remaining Communists with crimes, imprisoned them, and seized their property. Yeltsin also insisted upon changing names, signs, images, and other reminders of Soviet Russia. Putin, on the contrary, maintained that the Communist regime was a vital part of Russia's history and must be respected. Despite their injustices and transgressions, Putin believed that the Communists should be acknowledged for their contributions, refusing to continue unwarranted attacks against Communist leaders. Furthermore, Putin allowed several old Soviet symbols to return. The red military flag, the Soviet Star crest, and the Soviet national anthem have been resurrected, although the anthem's lyrics have been revised. Critics have alleged that Putin is catering to the Communists and not presenting a strong enough front for modern Russia. In response, Putin has asserted that he is the president of all Russians, including the Communists and those who lived in Soviet Russia and still remember and uphold its former glories.

Some critics asserted that Putin had unfairly removed potential political rivals and acted out of bounds. Others maintained that his goal was to reclaim big business from power-hungry, greedy oligarchs. Amid these arguments, the Russian public seemed satisfied that the corruptive powers and influences of the oligarchs had been destroyed.

Despite Boris Yeltsin's ties to the oligarchs—some of whom contributed large sums of money to his presidential re-election campaign—Putin granted him a complete pardon for any and all wrongdoings, making Yeltsin immune from prosecution. Many argue that he issued this pardon in return for gaining the presidency through Yeltsin. On the other hand, Putin claims that his predecessor is essentially a moral individual and does not deserve to be hounded.

KEY RESPONSES TO SEPTEMBER 11

On September 11, 2001, terrorists took control of four American passenger planes, using them to attack strategic buildings in New York City and outside Washington, D.C. In the D.C. attack, the plane struck the Pentagon, partially destroying it. In New York, two planes crashed into the World Trade Center, collapsing both of its landmark twin towers. Another plane, presumably aimed at the White House, crashed in a field in rural Pennsylvania. In total, nearly 3,000 people died, leaving the entire nation in shock.

Putin was the first foreign leader to call President George W. Bush, within hours of the attacks. The Russian president later appeared on television, telling the world that his country understood the dangers of terrorism and sympathized with the American people. When the United States announced its plan to attack the al Qaeda terrorist network in Afghanistan, Putin offered additional support, promising to provide Russian intelligence on the terrorists and permitting U.S. forces to use former Soviet bases. Never before had such a high degree of cooperation taken place between the two nations.

Putin has remarked that September 11 was a turning point in Russian foreign relations. His actions won the respect and support of the United States and many other countries. Among other benefits, Putin was able to secure President Bush's approval for a key arms reduction treaty, advance Russia's role in NATO, and establish the country as an auxiliary energy supplier to the United Sates and other Western nations.

MEDIA CONTROL

One benefit Putin's administration gained from dismantling the power of the oligarchs was the return of the media to state control. When Putin became president, only three television networks were large enough to influence the Russian people: ORT, RTR, and NTV. RTR was state-run, Boris Berezovsky controlled ORT, and Vladimir Gusinsky owned NTV. The state took control of NTV when Gusinsky was arrested, and gained ORT when Berezovsky fled Russia.

Many critics felt this was the end of Russian free press. Under Gorbachev's glasnost, the public, critics, and the media had more openly expressed their views after decades of censorship. With control of all three major networks,

Putin can determine what appears on the air and can prevent the news programs from reporting what he finds objectionable. This also permits the government to dictate what information is available to the Russian public regarding current events.

INCREASING POWER

In 2003, Russia held its parliamentary elections. The United Russia Party won a majority of seats. Putin himself supported United, which now held two-thirds of parliament. Many believed that this would give Putin too much power, claiming that parliament would simply rubber-stamp any policy he proposed. Conversely, others argued that Unity won because it clearly represented the Russian people's current interests.

In late February 2004, Putin dismissed his entire cabinet. He also removed Mikhail Kasyanov from his role as prime minister, appointing Mikhail Fradkov to that post in March. Kasyanov had worked under Yeltsin and still believed in Yeltsin's

Wearing traditional Chinese silk coats, Vladimir Putin and U.S. president George W. Bush attend the 2001 Asia Pacific Economic Cooperation (APEC) summit in Shanghai on October 21, 2001.

ideas for the government. He and other Yeltsin supporters remaining in office had clashed many times with Putin's team of economic reformers. Putin claimed these dismissals were done in order to build a more efficient government, a move some critics scrutinized, as presidential elections were less than a month away.

CHAPTER FIVE

A RETURN TO OFFICE

P utin won the election primary easily in 2003, and his second presidential election, in March 2004, was also a clear victory. He had won in 2000 with only 53 percent of the vote, and this climbed to 71 percent in 2004. Critics and opponents complained that Putin controlled the press, which made it difficult for rivals to campaign effectively. The Organization for Security and Cooperation in Europe's Office for Democratic Institutions and Human Rights oversaw the actual election, however. It declared the election free and fair, guaranteeing that Putin had not cheated.

FOCUSED ON THE FUTURE

During his first presidential term, Putin had cleaned house. He had restructured the government to provide more accountability and communication, removed many corrupt officials, broken the oligarchs' powers, reclaimed several

At a polling station, a woman in Baltiysk casts her vote during the presidential election on March 14, 2004. President Putin was running for his second term.

industries, and reinvigorated the nation's economy. Now that he was back in office and very popular, it was time to move forward.

Putin once described the four-year term as a year-by-year plan, in which dealing with corruption and setting up programs, administering these programs, studying their effectiveness, and reporting the studies' results and campaigning for re-election were each year-long activities. But this time, with the oligarchs gone, Putin had less corruption to address and would not be campaigning again—the Russian presidency only allows two four-year terms per individual. Therefore, during his second term, Putin has more time to concentrate on long-term plans and focus on Russia's future.

THE BESLAN SCHOOL CRISIS

On September 1, 2004, a group of heavily armed men and women seized a middle school in the North Ossetia town of Beslan. It was the first day of school, and returning and new students were there with their parents and siblings. The terrorists captured more than 1,100 hostages, most of them children. All cell phones were removed and the hostages were herded into the gym, which was then wired with explosives. The terrorists were apparently Islamic militants; North Ossetia is predominantly Orthodox Christian, and its neighboring territories are predominantly Muslim.

Armed soldiers in Beslan watch the school where Chechen separatists hold students and parents hostage on September 3, 2004, the third and last day of the crisis.

The Russian government stated that it would not use force in this situation because it was afraid of placing the hostages at risk. The terrorists had warned that they would kill fifty hostages for every one of them killed, and twenty hostages for every one of them hurt. The terrorists also selected the twenty strongest-looking male hostages and executed them, dumping their bodies outside.

A negotiator was sent to speak with the terrorists and managed to win one concession: some nursing mothers and their infants were released. Otherwise, negotiations failed. The government refused to give the terrorists food or water in an effort to invoke their surrender. Instead, many children fainted from the heat, thirst, hunger, and being held captive in such close quarters.

On the third day, servicemen (as part of the negotiations) were sent to remove the bodies from in front of the school. Gunfire erupted as they approached, then an explosion rocked the school. Believing that the hostage situation had reached a dire now or never, the government sent in troops, blowing holes in the wall to help the hostages escape. The gym was completely destroyed, most of it having caught fire.

More than 340 civilians died, about half of whom were children, and more than 500 were injured. The first explosion was later proved to be caused unintentionally. One of the terrorists' bombs had been poorly rigged, so it fell and exploded. In addition, the perpetrators of the siege were initially unknown, until Chechen guerrilla leader Shamil Basayev claimed responsibility.

As the entire nation mourned, Putin appeared on television on September 4. He mourned the loss of life and admitted that serious errors had been committed on the government's behalf. He also warned that Russia had been weak since the fall of the Soviet Union. "Weak people are beaten," he pointed out, arguing that Russia needed stronger security and better methods of defense.

Many criticized the Russian government for its handling of the situation, arguing that too much force was used, putting the hostages at risk. They also objected to the government's slow response, the lack of information available, and Putin's decision to close North Ossetia's borders during the crisis.

APPOINTING GOVERNORS

On September 13, less than two weeks after the Beslan crisis, Putin announced a new plan. He felt that the current regional governors were vulnerable, inclined to be corrupt, and should be removed from power. However, these officials could remain in office by controlling their regions and rigging elections in their favor. Therefore, Putin proposed to replace the election system altogether and presidentially appoint each region's governor instead. His appointments would have to be ratified by each region's legislature, but it was unlikely they would oppose his choices.

Many viewed this as a major step away from democracy. Many critics argued that this made Putin a dictator rather than a democratic leader, evoking objections from Gorbachev and Yeltsin. Putin countered these allegations with the argument that, due to recent events, a strong central government was essential in securing Russia's stability and creating a political climate favorable to more democratic methods.

The same day, Putin announced a change in the Duma, the lower house of Russia's parliament. Before, Duma deputies were appointed through a party system. More powerful parties won additional seats during the elections, but smaller parties that did not get any votes were still entitled to at least one seat. Putin changed this so that Duma members would be elected based purely on population and votes; parties without votes would not get any seats, resulting in fewer parties in parliament and more power for those that remained. Since Unity dominated the parliament, Putin's supporters would become more powerful.

In opposition, critics and Putin's opponents alleged that he was using the Beslan incident to further his own agenda. They accused Putin of consolidating power and reducing autonomy. Putin replied that these changes were necessary to protect and strengthen Russia's government.

THE UKRAINE PRESIDENTIAL ELECTION CONTROVERSY

Ukraine's presidential election of November 2004 caught a great deal of international attention. Prime Minister Viktor Yanukovych was running against former prime minister and opposition

leader Viktor Yushchenko. Russia strongly supported Yanukovych. Yushchenko was more liberal and more Western-thinking, and not surprisingly, this had earned him support from the United States and the European Union (EU).

Putin and other leaders anticipated the negative effects that Yushchenko's possible presidency would have on Russia. They feared losing the Common Economic Space established between Russia, Ukraine, Belarus, and Kazakhstan. Yushchenko was more likely to bring the Ukraine into NATO and the EU.

The first election was held on October 31. Yanukovych and Yushchenko each won 39 percent of the vote, but a candidate needed 50 percent to win. A runoff election was called for November 21. On November 23, Ukraine's

Ukraine president Viktor Yushchenko *(right)* congratulates Viktor Yanukovych on being appointed his prime minister by the Ukrainian parliament on August 4, 2006.

electoral commission reported that Yanukovych had won, with 49.42 percent of the vote. But observers for the Organization for Security and Cooperation in Europe said the election had not been fair. Other observers and politicians also claimed it had been rigged. Regions where Yanukovych was strong had shown significant increases in their votes for this election. On the other hand, reduced votes were shown in regions where Yushchenko held control. Putin had even congratulated Yanukovych on his victory—before the election results were in.

On December 2, Putin met with then Ukrainian President Leonid Kuchma, and they agreed that the elections should be repeated altogether. There had been twenty-six candidates on the original ballot, but the runoff had been between only Yanukovych and Yushchenko. A new election with all twenty-six candidates back on the ballot, would mean the votes would be spread out among everyone again, making it more difficult for anyone to gain the majority needed to win.

The Ukrainian Supreme Court did not agree.
On December 3, it called for a repeat of the
runoff election only. The second runoff was held
on December 26, and observers reported a much
fairer process. Yushchenko won 52 percent of
the vote. Yanukovych conceded on December 21
and resigned as prime minister the same day. He
appealed the election results, but his appeal was
rejected on January 6. Yushchenko was finally
sworn in on January 23, 2005.

Many nations criticized Russia's participation
in the process. They felt Putin and his officials
had aided Yanukovych in cheating. Moreover,
Yushchenko had also suffered from dioxin
poisoning. He fell ill after an official dinner on
September 5, 2004. One of the other attendees
was General Ihor P. Smeshko, head of Ukraine's
state police, formerly part of the KGB. Many
accused Smeshko, and Russia, of poisoning
Yushchenko, though this has never been proven.
Regardless, it is generally viewed that Putin had
not handled the situation well, as his support of
Yushchenko had been clumsy and ill-timed—it

took him a month to congratulate the new Ukrainian president on his victory.

With Yushchenko in office, Ukraine became less aligned with Russia and more interested in working with the rest of Europe and gaining membership to the EU. Meanwhile, Russia and other nations may form an alternative to the Common Economic Space—with or without the Ukraine.

UNPOPULAR PENSION REFORM

At the start of 2005, Putin introduced a plan to change pension benefits. For decades, pensioners had received free medicine, free or reduced-cost public transportation, and reduced-rate housing. Putin eliminated all of those benefits and replaced them with direct cash payments. He also established a system to get those payments out quickly. Many retirees vigorously opposed these changes.

Putin had stated before that he felt the former pension system was inefficient. He had cited the example of free transportation for the military. The law provided it, but Putin said few military

Relations with Syria

In February 2005, Putin met with President Bush in Bratislava. The two leaders agreed to cooperate in securing nuclear weapons and material, signing a cooperation agreement that requires them to share nuclear security management. They also agreed to work on using low-enriched uranium in their reactors. However, one of their dividing topics of discussion was the man-portable air defense system (MANPADS), a shoulder-fired anti-aircraft missile. Russia planned to sell MANPADS to Syria, and the United States was apprehensive that the weapons could then be transferred to terrorist groups. Putin refused to budge, however. He and Syrian President Bashar Assad met the previous month and had renegotiated Syria's debts. Putin had promised that Russia would sell Syria MANPADS, in return for Syria's guarantee that it would repay $1.5 billion of its remaining debt in cash over the next decade. Also, Putin and Assad had agreed that the rest of the debt would be invested in joint projects within Syria. That April, Putin confirmed this MANPADS sale, upsetting both the United States and Israel.

On September 22, 2005, the day after the parliamentary vacation, the fall session of the Duma commences with the Duma deputies listening to the national anthem.

officials actually received such a benefit—they usually had to pay for their transportation. Putin maintained that it would be advantageous to raise salaries and pension amounts and remove the previous laws and benefits, which he felt were largely unobserved or cumbersome.

Pensioners disagreed, asserting that the new pension amount was not enough to cover medicine, housing, and transportation—all three had been accessible through the previous system. In response, Putin agreed to raise the monthly pension amount, blaming local and federal officials for not making the transition to the new pension system smoother. Ultimately, however, he argued that the former system could not be restored, as providing such benefits were no longer affordable for the government.

Putin's reform of the pension system adversely affected his popularity. His approval rating plummeted and mass protests occurred. His supporters claimed political rivals were organizing the protests, but in reality, the vast majority of protesters were pensioners. This has been Putin's most unpopular move to date, as retirees are one of his strongest potential power bases, making up 40 million votes.

THE "GREATEST" CATASTROPHE

On April 25, 2005, Putin spoke to the Federal Assembly. During the televised speech, Putin stated the collapse of the Soviet Union was "the greatest geopolitical catastrophe of the century." People around the world and in Russia felt this statement was inappropriate. It seemed as if Putin expressed a desire for the return of the Soviet Union and lamented its loss. Putin claimed that his words were misconstrued, assuring the public that he did not yearn for the ways of Communist Russia and had not meant to place the dissolution of the USSR in a conclusively negative light. Instead, Putin insisted that he was referring to the dramatic impact its collapse had upon the world, and particularly how strongly it had affected Russia and the other former Soviet republics.

CHAPTER SIX

THE FACE OF RUSSIAN LEADERSHIP

Putin has now been president for two terms. In that time, he has gone from a virtual unknown to the established face of Russian leadership. His name, face, and voice are known around the world and his opinion carries great weight among the world's leaders. But what do they really think of him?

AN AUTOCRAT

Many accuse Putin of being an autocrat, a dictator. They allege that he has exploited events of the past few years, particularly the ongoing Chechen crisis, to consolidate power for himself. These critics believe Putin ultimately wants control of Russia from top to bottom, driven by personal ambition rather than the country's interests.

Putin disagrees, of course. He has stated many times that he is not interested in power or its privileges. Putin projects an image very different from the traditional dictator, who lives

Shown on two huge screens, Vladimir Putin addresses the opening session of the tenth summit of the Organization of the Islamic Conference (OIC) in Putrajaya, Malaysia, on October 16, 2003.

luxuriously at the cost of the public. His life outside the presidency, from his personal taste to his family's estate, reflects moderation instead of indulgence. Furthermore, instead of accumulating wealth unscrupulously through the oligarchs like numerous Russian politicians, Putin doggedly pursued them to end their influence on politics.

Amid accusations of centralizing state power for his own ends, Putin responds that he implemented these measures because Russia, while beset by internal conflict and corruption, is not able to handle such liberal policies. In several instances, he has even expressed regret for resorting to the consolidation of powers. Moreover, Putin has made assurances that the reigns of the central government will be loosened once Russia's stability has been achieved.

AN ANTI-DEMOCRAT

When Putin first became president, much of the global community, including many Western nations, believed that Russia finally had a solid, thoroughly competent leader. Despite Gorbachev's leading role in ending the Cold War, his sweeping liberal policies of perestroika and glasnost had backfired. Then, Yeltsin's bold, if erratic, leadership had allowed oligarchs to take political prominence, and his economic reforms had floundered. Putin, on the other hand, exhibited quiet resolve and steely focus, and arrived with an agenda that was anti-corruption and economically sound. During his first presidential term, he eliminated the corrupted business and political inner circles and helped to turn the Russian economy around. Western leaders applauded these actions.

During his second term, however, Putin has appointed governors instead of electing them, wants oversight on judges, and has eliminated smaller parties from Duma representation. More and more, Putin has taken direct control of processes within the government.

Nor have the changes stopped with the government. Putin has seized control of the major Russian television networks, blocked newspapers and other reporters, and censored or banned reports. Freedom of the press, which began with Gorbachev and flourished under Yeltsin, is argued to be vanishing rapidly.

Big business has begun to suffer as well. Putin has accused the oligarchs of corruption and has seized many of their assets, which have then been claimed by the state. Many of Russia's largest industries are now state-run again, just as they were under the Communist regime of the old Soviet Union.

Some critics say Putin is anti-democratic. They accuse him of deliberately stripping away the people's freedoms and returning the nation to the days of rigid control, repression, and individual inaction.

Putin rigorously counters these allegations. He admits that he has acted to consolidate state power, but that it is for the long-term interest of Russia. According to Putin, Russia must become a democratic nation gradually, and both Gorbachev and Yeltsin hastily pursued this process. Putin is determined to learn from his predecessors' errors and proceed with the democratization of Russia with caution by first laying the groundwork for political and economic stability.

Putin has also been accused of returning to old KGB practices of killing critics and rivals. Ukrainian President Yushchenko claims to be one of Putin's victims, though the dioxin poisoning failed to kill him. Former FSB (the successor of the KGB) Colonel Alexander Litvinenko and

Alexander Litvinenko *(right)* and a masked colleague attend a news conference on November 17, 1998, when Litvinenko was colonel of the Federal Security Service, Russia's current intelligence agency.

investigative journalist Anna Politkovskaya were not as lucky. Both were outspoken critics of Putin's policies and died under mysterious circumstances. Politkovskaya was fatally shot in Moscow in October 2006, and Litvinenko, who fled to London with his family in 1990, died in November 2006 of radiation poisoning. Putin claims his administration has no involvement in either death and has publicly extended his regrets to both families. Investigations so far have not proven that Putin is linked to these assassinations.

A RELIGIOUS MAN

Putin is openly religious. He has embraced the Russian Orthodox church and attends confession regularly. Many of his top advisors and aides are Orthodox, too. It is even alleged that Putin had insisted a new aide be baptized before working with him.

Religious faith is unusual among recent Russian leaders. For many, like Yeltsin, attending church was likely a superficial demonstration of religiousness. Putin, however, is genuinely, if discreetly, devout, remaining silent about his relationship with his confessor and religious practices. Also, he has not pushed religion upon anyone or the public, except perhaps the aforementioned aide.

Nonetheless, Putin's rise to power has seen an increase in Russian religion. More people are attending church. More are also being baptized into the Russian Orthodox church, including adults. Many Russian churches now have adult-sized baptismal fonts to accommodate such converts.

Many regard Putin's faith as an asset. He has not shown any anti-Semitic tendencies, as numerous Russian leaders have in the past. In fact, he has met with several Russian Jewish leaders and worked to help them overcome long-standing difficulties. Putin has a somewhat conflicted view of Islam, perhaps due to the crisis in Chechnya and its Islamic insurgents.

While some adults are converting to Orthodoxy, far more children and teenagers are entering the church. The Kremlin has even organized a youth group, Idushie Vmeste ("Moving Together"). Members are all church-goers who help at orphanages and promote classic Russian literature. They hand out crosses at street corners and speak openly against abortion—Russia's abortion rate is among the highest in the world. Idushie Vmeste supports both Putin and the church, meaning Putin or his successors will have a strong power base when these children are old enough to vote themselves.

A RUSSIAN

First and foremost, Putin is a Russian. He is fiercely loyal to his country and has a passion for Russian history and law. Therefore, he has cultivated a strong understanding of Russia's past, which is a fundamental reason why he argues that it is not yet prepared for a fully democratized government. According to Putin, Russia is a historically paternalistic state, meaning it was traditionally governed by a political leader who singularly acted as a father figure. He asserts that the Russian people still need a governing body that resembles a paternalistic state. Until the nation has moved beyond this dependence, Putin believes that liberalized policies will continue to fail.

Putin is convinced that a Western-style economy would not succeed in Russia. Although he desires the establishment of a strong market economy, he argues that it must be compatible with Russia's preexisting economy. Putin believes one of the Yeltsin administration's most serious errors was attempting to apply

As a symbol of France's closeness to Russia, Vladimir Putin receives the Legion of Honor rosette from French president Jacques Chirac during their meeting in Paris on September 22, 2006.

Western economic concepts without adapting them to the economic structures that have long been established in Russia.

Despite being a reserved individual who supposedly shuns attention, Putin has proven to be a powerful speaker. He also has solid relationships with numerous key world leaders such as President Bush, French President Jacques Chirac, former Italian Prime Minister Silvio Berlusconi, and former German Chancellor Gerhard Schröder. Furthermore, he has maintained amicable relations among countries such as Israel and Syria. Putin has made no secret of his goal in these relationships; he is working to improve Russia's global profile and establish strong foreign ties.

A NATIONAL FATHER FIGURE

Russia's constitution limits a president to two four-year terms of office. Putin's second term ends in March of 2008. But will he leave? Many predict he will amend the constitution or devise a plan to extend his presidency. Presently, Putin does not face the threat of removal from office, and some believe that his administration could continue beyond its two-term limit without critical or sustained objections. Some might even welcome his continued leadership, as Putin wrought significant changes in Russia during his presidency. Some of his reforms have had immediate positive results. Others have seemed negative at the time, but could prove beneficial in the long run.

Even if Putin does leave office, he still yields tremendous influence on Russia's future, as Putin will have the opportunity to appoint a successor. The people will vote, of course, but the current president's support carries a great deal of weight. Whether Putin will endorse either Sergei Ivanov or Dimitri Medvedev as his successor is currently under speculation. Both are deputy prime ministers in his government, and Putin has known and trusted them for years. One of Putin's political rivals, Mikhail Kasyanov, has already declared that he will run in 2008. Kasyanov was Putin's prime minister until February 2004 and has been one of Putin's most outspoken critics since. However, Putin still controls most of Russia's television and news, and whomever he endorses will have access to the media for his campaigns. That could make all the difference.

Putin's influence may extend well after the election of his successor. He has a long, deep

The Chechnya Crisis

Unfortunately, the Chechnya crisis continues. In 1994, Russia invaded Chechnya to prevent radical separatist Dzhokhar Dudayev from gaining control and establishing an independent nation. The fighting continued for two years, until Dudayev was assassinated. As a consequence, his followers established a truce with Russia. But in 1999, the guerrilla leader Shamil Basayev invaded neighboring Dagestan, intending to unite Chechnya and Dagestan into an independent Islamic state. Days after this invasion, Putin became prime minister and immediately sent in troops to drive the rebels out of Dagestan. He also invaded Chechnya and bombed its capital, Grozny. The fighting has continued since and shows no sign of abating. The majority of Russians no longer want to be entrenched in violence with the Chechen rebels. Putin also wants an end to the violence, but has expressed that he will not be satisfied with anything less than Russian victory and will not cease military actions in Chechnya until the rebels have completely surrendered. Ultimately, he wants to provide them with Russian leadership until a Chechen leader can be elected fairly and without incident.

Members of the Kremlin-sponsored youth group Idushie Vmeste celebrate the second anniversary of their group's formation on May 7, 2002. It has almost 100,000 members throughout Russia.

political involvement in both Moscow and St. Petersburg, and he counts many influential figures as his friends and allies. Moreover, emerging leaders and politicians will inevitably turn to him for his opinions. To varying degrees, Gorbachev and Yeltsin's opinions of current affairs are still sought and taken into consideration, and Putin would join them as an unofficial advisor. His endorsement could convince legislators to vote on a particular motion or program, while his disapproval could cause them to vote against it.

No matter what happens, Putin's administration has already shaped the development of post-Soviet Russia. Given enough time, Putin could become the stern father figure he feels Russia needs for guidance—in or out of office.

TIMELINE

1952 October 7, Vladimir Putin is born in Leningrad.

1966 Putin begins studying judo.

1970 Putin graduates high school. He is accepted to Leningrad State University.

1975 Putin graduates with a degree in law from Leningrad State University and reports to the KGB.

1983 Putin marries Lyudmila Aleksandrovna.

1985 Putin and Lyudmila are sent to Dresden, East Germany. Their daughter Masha is born.

1986 Daughter Katya is born.

1990 Putin returns to St. Petersburg and becomes an advisor to Anatoly Aleksandrovich Sobchak, the chairman of the Leningrad City Council.

1991 Putin becomes chairman of the St. Petersburg City Council's International Relations Committee.

1992 Putin becomes first deputy chairman of the St. Petersburg city government (first deputy mayor).

1996 June, Sobchak loses the mayoral election in St. Petersburg. Putin resigns as first deputy mayor.

1996 August, Putin is appointed deputy head of the president's Administrative Directorate. He and his family move to Moscow.

1997 Putin becomes deputy head of the Executive Office of the President (Presidential Administration).

1998 May, Putin is promoted to first deputy head of the Presidential Administration.

1998 July, Putin is appointed director of the Federal Security Service.

1999 March, Putin becomes secretary of the Security Council.

1999 August, Putin is appointed prime minister.

1999 December 31, Boris Yeltsin resigns. Putin becomes acting president.

2000 Putin is elected president of Russia. He is inaugurated on May 7, 2000.

2004 March 14, Putin is elected president of Russia for the second term.

2007 Putin vows to remain "an influence" in Russia even after leaving office in 2008.

Glossary

anti-Semitic Someone or something (like a law) that is specifically biased against Jews.

autocrat An absolute ruler.

banya A Russian steam bath.

baptismal font A cistern filled with holy water for baptizing children.

Berlin Wall A wall that literally divided the city of Berlin into its East German and West German halves. It was dismantled in 1989.

Communism A political philosophy that puts the people and the workers first, holds that all property is shared by everyone, and believes that everyone puts in as much effort as they can and takes out what they need.

coup When one person or a group of people attempt to take control of their own government and replace the current leaders.

Duma The Russian parliament.

enigma Something mysterious and unexplained.

Federal Security Service (FSB) Russia's intelligence agency.

Federation Council The upper house of Duma.

FRG The Federal Republic of Germany, or West Germany.

GDR The German Democratic Republic, or East Germany.

glasnost Mikhail Gorbachev's policy for increased economic participation, regulation, and debate through transparency and free speech, meaning "openness" and "publicity."

Idushie Vmeste A pro-Putin Russian Orthodox youth group, meaning "moving together."

judo A Japanese martial art and philosophy, meaning "gentle way."

KGB The Komitet Gosudarstvennoy Bezopasnosti (the Committee of State Security), the former Soviet Union's intelligence agency.

Kremlin Russia's executive government headquarters, equivalent to the United States' White House.

NATO The North Atlantic Treaty Organization; it aims to protect the security of Europe and North America.

oligarch A powerful businessman; particularly one of the Russian businessmen who rose to power after Yeltsin's presidency.

perestroika Mikhail Gorbachev's extensive plans for liberalizing Russian economic policies, meaning "restructuring."

pragmatist A practical, realistic person.

Russian Orthodox Church A Russian denomination of Christianity, also known as the Orthodox Catholic Church of Russia.

sambo A Soviet martial art that combines judo and wrestling.

Stasi The East German secret police.

USSR The United Soviet Socialist Republics, or Soviet Union, a former nation and former world superpower dissolved in 1991.

Warsaw Pact An organization of Central and Eastern European Communist states.

Young Pioneers The Lenin All-Union Pioneer Organization, a Soviet youth organization, designed to make children good Soviet citizens.

For More Information

Embassy of the Russian Federation
2650 Wisconsin Avenue NW
Washington, DC 2007
(202) 298-5735
Web site: http://www.russianembassy.org/

President of Russia
Presidential Executive Office
4, Staraya Square
Moscow, 103132, Russia
Web site: http://www.kremlin.ru/eng

Russian Cultural Heritage Network (RCHN)
Dept. 110, Vavilova St. 57
State Darwin Museum
Moscow, 117292, Russia
Web site: http://www.rchn.org.ru

Russian Union of Youth (RUY)
RUY Central Committee

Maroseika, 3/13
Moscow, 101990, Russia
Web site: http://www.ruy.ru/pages.asp?cid=17

Samara Regional Democratic Movement
PROGRESSIVE YOUTH UNION
196 Molodogvardeyskaya Ul.
Samara, 443001, Russia
Web site: http://www.samara.org/english.htm

WEB SITES

Due to the changing nature of Internet links, Rosen Publishing has developed an online list of Web sites related to the subject of this book. This site is updated regularly. Please use this link to access the list:

http://www.rosenlinks.com/nm/vlpu

For Further Reading

Ascher, Abraham. *Russia: A Short History.*
Oxford, England: Oneworld Publications, 2002.

Corona, Laurel. *Former Soviet Republics—
The Russian Federation.* New York, NY:
Lucent, 2001.

Lange, Brenda, Charles J. Shields, and Arthur
Meier Schlesinger. *Vladimir Putin* (Major
World Leaders), 2nd ed. New York, NY:
Chelsea House Publications, 2007.

Putin, Vladimir, *First Person: An Astonishingly Frank
Self-Portrait by Russia's President.* New York,
NY: PublicAffairs, 2000.

Schmemann, Serge. *When the Wall Came Down:
The Berlin Wall and the Fall of Soviet
Communism.* New York, NY: Kingfisher, 2006.

Shulman, Sol. *Kings of the Kremlin: Leaders from
Ivan the Terrible to Boris Yeltsin.* London,
England: Brassey's UK, 2003.

Stoff, Laurie. *The Rise and Fall of the Soviet Union* (Opposing Viewpoints in World History). San Diego, CA: Greenhaven Press, 2005.

Streissguth, Thomas. *Vladimir Putin*. New York, NY: First Avenue Editions, 2005.

Bibliography

Dougherty, Jill. "9/11 a 'Turning Point' for Putin." CNN.com. September 10, 2002. Retrieved October 15, 2006 (http://archives.cnn.com/2002/WORLD/europe/09/10/ar911.russia.putin/).

Encyclopedia Britannica. "Union of Soviet Socialists Republics." Retrieved December 13, 2006 (http://www.search.eb.com/eb/article-9105999).

Fontaine, Roger. "Getting a Sense of Putin's Soul." *Washington Times.* April 17, 2005, pp. B05–B07.

Goldgeier, James M., and Michael Mcfaul. "What to Do About Russia." *Policy Review.* No. 133, 2005.

Kurlantzick, Joshua. "The Rise and Fall of Imperial Democracies: From the Beltway to Bangkok, Moscow to Manila, Elected Leaders Are Using the Threat of Terror to Grab More Power—and Making the Threat Worse." *Washington Monthly.* Vol. 38, January–February 2006, pp. 33–40.

Lloyd, John. "Is Russia Closing in on Itself Again?" *New Statesman.* Vol. 132, January 27, 2003, pp. 22–25.

Putin, Vladimir. *First Person: An Astonishingly Frank Self-Portrait by Russia's President Vladimir Putin.* New York, NY: Public Affairs, 2000.

Sands, David R. "Putin Strengthens Power at Cost of Popular Support; Takes Hits for Pension Reform." *Washington Times.* February 3, 2005, p. A15.

Solomon Jr., Peter H. "Vladimir Putin's Quest for a Strong State." *International Journal on World Peace.* Vol. 22, 2005, pp. 3–6.

Starobin, Paul. "The Accidental Autocrat." *Atlantic Monthly.* Vol. 295, March 2005.

Washington Times. "Which Direction for Putin?" February 26, 2005, p. A12.

Index

ABOUT THE AUTHOR

Aaron Rosenberg's maternal great-grandparents fled Russia at the start of the twentieth century to escape Jewish prosecution, which accounts for his personal interest in Russia's history. Currently, he lives with his wife and children in New York City.

PHOTO CREDITS

Cover, cover background, pp. 5, 40, 43, 49, 51, 54, 59, 65, 74, 80, 84, 88, 92 © AFP/Getty Images; p. 10 © AP/Wide World Photos; pp. 14, 36, 67, 69 © Getty Images; pp. 20, 27, 96 © TASS/Sovfoto; p. 33 © Time-Life Pictures/Getty Images.

Designer: Gene Mollica; **Editor:** Roman Espejo
Photo Researcher: Marty Levick